48 SMALL POEMS

48
SMALL
POEMS

MARC WEBER

University of ⌇
Pittsburgh Press

ISBN 0–8229–3257–1 (cloth)
ISBN 0–8229–5234–3 (paper)
Copyright © 1973, Marc Weber
All rights reserved
Media Directions Inc., London
Manufactured in the United States of America

To Linda, Guy, and Tom

CONTENTS

48 SMALL POEMS

1   what are the values oh but
    I want to feel someone says I
    want to know

    sense of wonder never gone
    always that taste no matter
    how far degeneration

    involved in entropy I say
    to myself and then pick up
    my book again

2 night came and bats skimmed the
surface reflections into the lighter
sky chilling air and stillness my father
keeps throwing his line again and again
he says he may catch a bat but
they do not come too near
no hooked insect on a line for them
no posts that speak either
even though we speak softly
across the lake a fish splashes as
it is drawn its belly shows and it
is lifted up and taken the bats draw
my attention they are silent to my ears
they ride the air between the hills
that make this valley quiet
still like the water between the reeds
they take their food without disturbance
they are something to remember and my father
who is he my father his moustache and tanned face
and hands in his plaid shirt standing to
take down his pole my father asks me
to carry it back for him

3 honestly there are many things to say
and the many lips that speak
them will not stop all is said in
little pieces one at a time
that look to be true but aren't
or are and the words are
patented even though who spoke them
is a spark

words are bits of sparks they
all are too much alike
alike with all and so blows
death yes excuse me for it's tired

blowing came up because of the
wind outside. so what? haven't
written for days what can I give
but facts I'm out of practice
at other things

but the wind is blowing
and I've been talking many
times today about Our Fate
it's a major topic lately
what concern it is
is everybody's and
nobody's of course I know
(don't you guess it) what my
Fate is or I think so since it's
here already just in these words

4 I suppose everything I am will come
out whether or not I intend to inject it into
your mind and all that I want you to
be like me in will be shown to you
by the smallest glance and turn of face
and phrase it is impossible to hide anything
and my inanity doesn't help my telling you
what way to live

5 mother used to have simple faith positive
   optimist common morals trust in God
   still has a portrait of Christ hanging in
   the living room now she says her head's
   full of theories and no beliefs other than
   her saying that she's not changed ·in the slightest
   and still has a common morality
   expects the same from her sons common goodness
   that's all no ambitious mother
   'you're no genius,' she said to me, in her tone
   it said, 'and I don't want you to be'
   just don't be nasty don't lie to her
   don't ride a motorcycle drive race cars
   or fly in small planes

8 rich building and young skins young hair
young faces and old books stacked above the
bright new carpet with the young bodies throughout
the building and quiet with no windows
buzzing neons throughout the open hall-less
architecture and lonely in the rows
of books

9 the warmest night passing
solitary music comes from the house
across the way some old master
all the stars gleam as the heavy basses
keep up time the flutes come back and I
imagine nights in Vienna

going to the bathroom the phone rings
someone there? she says, no you have the wrong no.
I lay the receiver down no good-bye farewell
and make my way on
typical sounds and I return no more
records it's as silent out there
as usual no good-byes either

10 a while back Bermuda I remember
I wrote of a girl who is there or
I think is there now that I once
knew once knew never see again
unless the world is as close and the
millions of faces are as close
as my mind, and the teeming millions
and she is lost among them for I do not
seek her but only remember

11 I've released that golden spinner
back I've speared it through
the water and hooked in the
calm behind the log a tension
straining for life
driving in the high mountain
passes and treeless summits
gray and cool
snow-patched and then the
memory by the stream that time
with boulders buried in their ground
behind me

12 lone walker dressed in
a drab green coat and
corduroys walking up toward
the library the wind has died down
and there are no cars
almost sundown everything is
in the lurch I watch you from my
window ascend the hill I
know your name

poem on his birthday

13 not in the sky not even
if we enter into the midst of the sea
or the clefts of mountains is there
a place to avoid death said Gotama
like a shattered gong you
utter nothing then Nirvana men
are driven by age and death
like cows before the drover he said
later or sometime and he surprised
me with his words for I know
death is not that important but he
did know others like me
and used to be others so he spoke
a few words in passing that I thought about
now as I am writing beside the words
and being warmed by the covers I am
under it is now a little past my birthday
that was just before the minute hand moved
by midnight
                    20 years old however long now

14 in the universe and the dark auditorium
moons and lights finally dimming
down down into make-believe
and the film speaks of death over
and over in the universe of the film
voices and music writhing scenes
some of it's beautiful, at the end
death again but the lights come up
and I leave

in a hurry out into the real night
and heaven of stars may we please
relate to the end no says the monk
no for your end is so apparent
that speaking is but a vain labor

15

the small lapping wind
on the window and to look
out is only fair there
you are being blown to pieces
I'd better hurry and open the door

16

up by the grotto aspens were dense around its mouth
the sound of the river came from below, then the darkness
took it moss hung down black strings around the
mouth wet rock down below water in the depths
voices barely heard in whispers to get out

back down to the sand, up across the footbridge.
smoke is coming from before the tent
smell the bacon

17 speaking on and on in the conversation
on the artists' works in the small office
then he quoted something
after a while reading aloud from an old book
he laughs as a point of errata is
encountered so funny these old lit. editors
and the room stacked with books
of letters and print ink smelling of the ink
and lines of thousands of block-set
letters of the yellowed pages

Dr Faustus

18 in the heat of summer now and
without break from the heat the day
goes to night we wait and listen
talk about Dr Faustus watch him
burn in hell all the talk about the earth
in the center of all the straightforward
surety only mystery in the frame-
work of things only self-doubt
not unknowing about all God o
great Overlord of all without flaw to them
'the wages of sin is death' and the great
passion

then there was passion and being
cast into hell what horror he raged
with terror it was still hot when he
was over and burning gone down with
clinging Helen into the red pit I went out
on the dark porch by my father where it was cooler
and sat in the quiet and told him about
Marlowe and talked about the heat I heard
a helicopter passing and pointed out its
lights between the leafy branches the lights were
especially bright, since it was overcast
I did not feel at all attached to Faustus
he could not even make a decision and keep to it
his passion I recognized that I have none

19 what young mind working
with clear complexion somewhere alone
and kinetic strong and potent
spins the words that
are never heard

fresh creation unexpected
undreamed of that overshadows
all I have ever said and
she is one I know

20

am heading straight for it
  no longer a pause
    because of youth but onward

straight for what you keep going
or something keeps (what is you)
going you cannot be sad or happy
oh you can be (but can you be)
onward ever onward 'through time
like a diver,' you once said.

you once said.

21

prompting this the clouds of rain
or perhaps snow that conceal the light
and us the houses of the work force who have
not yet done
mean to stay to their laws and move and
dissipate when they will but the houses
of the work force have not yet done
windows dark and early twilight dark
for the clouds and silent to the afternoon
we know the zenith
has done the houses are on the new and damaged
earth that we have not done to the end

22

face sunken and grave
eyes between folds skin
in the sun of the open door
she sits on a high stool and
looks down at me she wears
no makeup whatsoever she is
not pretty but is something else
she is strong and speaks without
wavering eyes there is nothing
at all she is afraid of from me

23

what kind of man are you oh don't
say too much that someone else made up
for you to be don't say the words
of a philosopher who wrote about a Man
that exists for you in your memory of
his words but what are you without
words how do you react to
life how do you smile at a girl
what do you say without words, brave
or a coward a rogue or indifferent
to living, going along with it
intelligent in what and what are
you without a hundred books behind
you speaking speaking never
ceasing to say their words

when a little child who were you

"like water drops from a lotus leaf"

24

the mind runs off considering
the snow this night following
the light away and into the unilluminated
darkness beyond the tent
of light that slants from the street lamp
toward the dim lights of houses
and coming back again to the fine sleet
that drives down
following the light away into the
light of the mind beyond and
within the tent of light beyond
and within the silence and movement
of the sleet

25

automatons

making love drinking eating
sleeping smoking automatons

dying slowly in our brains
automatons of the age of
toxic pleasure

things in the air
things in the food
and we smoke and drink

or we self-restrain
automatons
nevertheless automatons

we make love
take the pill or do
not and we make
children automatons

incessantly articulate
automatons

REVOLUTIONISTS

26 have to be ready to die for it, she was saying
as we rode home from the meeting. a hundred miles.
she was in the front seat. I was in the back. she
was turned to me the headlights floated across
her face her eyes were black I could see
the shadow of my head I said, 'I'm not ready to
die for anything'

27

someone who asked me what I said to you
clouds in twilight breathing fumes I look up
through tinted glass at them green, long
and blown above where the mountain
stops and I had and have nothing to say to you
and if someone asks I am dumb
I am even numb to myself I have no respect
my feelings mean nothing to me even rationality
and empathy are cheapened I have no validity
my ruins are buried oh yes they are
let's get up and sing and sing of my ruins
my ruins are lovely and dark
and not so deep no not so deep

28

endless snow
for a full day snowflakes
endlessly big swirling coming
down unmelting
                white roads
coated branches in which the
birds perch between
the ridges of it below freezing how
do they survive. pair of sparrows
deformities on the top branches isolated
motionless
             endless snow

29

the pure mind, the source of everything,
resourceful in its form
untrackable in its reach
unlinkable to my
mouth

30 oh I've said I want to see the end
want to see the future want to see what happens
I expect an end to come for me to see
perhaps it won't come that soon
I've said I'd stay alive till then to see
it maybe stay alive until I've a B.A.
stay alive until something's completed

but soon we're there and finally
at no completion but a conclusion
a contusion a fracture a ripping
or breaking down quietly
violently burned
lying on my bed thinking about things
thinking about what I have to read
about what I wrote last time, feeling at
what might be written and wandering
at last toward emptiness
what about suicide die young then
nobody's disappointed
and one has to die written or unwritten
and then all is over a silence there
is met and I am at the fringe

sparkling neurons go no farther
electric visions go dark it's time
for action. is it. I do nothing.
finally I think about something else,
that I want to see the end and want to see the future
want to see what happens.

31 lie softly that is as the
body can and be comfortable
where you are we satiate and then we desire
again it is you again in the birds
outside through the gauze of
the curtains the tops of green trees
just sundown lie softly for a while

32

don't ask me any questions
since it has come time and now my
thoughts are not like before and the
day is meet in summer and all the people
are out on cycles this year healthier than
ever and young in the sunlight the girls
with muscular thighs hanging
down to the pedals
bare midriffs go by those I cannot stand
they assault me every moment
I see a girl riding by her
bare tan legs then past another girl
how many more

cycle

33 driving up the hill and the
blaze to my eyes when the top
falls below me and the town lights
are brilliant tonight as warm as
summer and perfect new Spring and
falling down without effort the
breeze meets my face and down
down back into the trees and darkness
mechanical solitude of
night the first meeting of skin and black
night breath speed on man breathed
this air this speed to the end throttling down

34 order is beauty in your
face and in the symmetry of eyes
that balances the intellect as
Buddha's face did not encumber him and
the middle way between your eyes
is a long path that I line with my
scanning that distance that is there
and the snowfields that lie upon the ridges
are no farther than the length
of the ways along the hollows of your cheeks

and order is beauty or a seeming
repose in the quiet of your flesh
beaming the sun rays

35

the open night and without passion
first night of Spring and without wind
facing a small park
the shapes of trees dark between the lighted
streets tall & massive aged pines

36   lines of vaporizing gray
and black even to me those clouds
to the mountains
mist and fog with lines
of their own magnitude such
wonders in a thousand years
I wonder your little lips
and eyes o man do you speak
to me do you want me to answer
you? do you? you want me
to obey your wish, bow to your
difference? and a thousand years
and even now the clouds

breakfast outside

37 early morning that's what everything is
and woman's hips viewed from behind
like hills and the dawn to rise
and the day the dawn
cold and wonderful early Spring eating
oatmeal a furnace steaming I wouldn't
feel cold not now

38

to be alone and undisputing
over any problem, not overcoming
obstacles of any kind, without
a means to give the feeling of
movement into the horizon within or without
but staying neither contracting nor
expanding where being alone
undisputing thinking it's time for
bed having done nothing all day feeling that
you can do nothing turning
to the lamp and applying a gentle
pressure at the last moment
before the night is let in giving up

39 little time enough for amnesia or am
I alive still this morning how can
I be alive and now I am to act this
morning alive now alive and time
to go now. now. and time to go
to rise the sun on my limbs and
alive the sun on my cheeks

40

all is fire Buddha said to
Ananda all is fire the eye is
on fire the nose is on fire the touch
is fire you are fire of
fire you are heat come to life burning
deeper

like burning nearer
in autumn after frost the
sun fire through closed
windows you through tight woolen
the touch is fire
and so is all life a slow chemical flame
crackling in time
     and heat you are or
     nothing more than flame
nothing less

Grandfather

41

yes I am descended from his loins it
is not to be denied and today he is stiff
and shrunken into an old decrepit man
living alone in a run-down house
with a rusted-out water heater and
tonight I went over and mopped
up his floor after searching around
and then forcing the main valve to turn
off he was sitting there with his
galoshes on staring at me through
thick glasses as I squeezed the water
into the bucket he and I are
not so very far apart

every lesson

42 and the brain, what are
you talking about? will you
get off it my old
man you have not seen the
sun in half of your years and
now you will not see it!
yes now what I have said to you
and brains crying out in
every moment of sparking in images
in phrases and sounds
voices of my parents images of
trees water rain streams fishing
girls along the way their
thighs every eye their faces
their mouths
brains sparking in every moment
old man brain sparking every
lesson: all the forms of earth

43

some age the brain dies as watching
young girls boy I've been watching them
my brain not yet dying I guess still
growing in me haven't read enough to know
these young legs are as cool a pale red
this summer as ever they could
be young I do not think about their
brains I'm as weak as Proust about
these girls
can I help it the brain dying without
help hundreds of neurons shall
die every day I will slowly be less
than the day before, an aging man
reading tracts a leaking cup
wanting to reach its brim yes it's
true

44 sometime before the end before we say
nothing at our good-bye before we part
you looking away from me and
then I turn also to somewhere
in time and space where you
will never be

somewhere in all
of it there must be an answer to the
question I must ask of what you feel
or don't for have you pretended

45

they expect about one hundred
or more selected works that will
encompass sufficent range
          and poem after poem should be
suitable on its own and every poem
should have blood and skin senses
sensibility so that it is explored to
a suitable level of quality and is endurable.
poem after poem turned loose
to live without me good-bye children
bastards that I leave with paper to
stay behind in other thoughts I have no more
of that time this poem gone

46

gaining nothing is that true are
you behind and losing ground
every day thinner hair fewer
cells I can feel it how can you . . .
I don't know perhaps I remember
something of the way thoughts used
to glide around one another
whatever it is something
remembered and gone
now my first love that is only
a half love and there is
nothing more to give

47

taking some very liberal interesting classes no exams
only chatty read-a-lots in a group
talking about the nature of man, nature
of university, nature of USA, nature
of good, nature of history and many
many digressions,
in passing and all a lot of work learning
a lot oh yes every day things to do
and then I'm asked to help put out a magazine
become a lit. editor all for art
all for art and learning, we're such
scholars

all the time we're learning, talking
so intellectual going to bed talking
about socialism, aesthetics, poetry-writing
metaphysics and then the lips stop
and come together, we're so
educated never want to stop

'have you read this book, it's worth reading'
so I read it give my opinion they say
yeah, yeah, and give theirs the week passes
in a flash the weekend arrives I still
feel it's Monday can't believe it
the moment
what do I have to do? check my mind
make a list head into time

we all want to learn we all read so much
and specialize get into it we all
know each other and give our minds
to the discussion of whatever we might be
on now and then we argue but
never bitterness

soon it will be over just as a week
has flashed just as everything has gone
only a few things remain
in my mind I started to write here
about learning and death a nice,
indirect poem with imagistic associations
to be relayed with contrasting words
for I would never speak about that
without the proper milieu
and of learning and death what can one
say, nothing new, but I have feelings about it
but how can one say those feelings
one can only give an impression of them
only a slight touch

48 after New Year's and I have
passed what probably is my last holiday with my parents
and my aunt and perhaps my brother (for quite
a while) do I have a haiku to write for
that is what I started here for

> white clouds in the sky
> that is evening and new year
> faces in the street voices

disconnected rambling like New Year's what
is appropriate to it nothing narrow
just fragmented life separate voices
faces everything broken Guy Lombardo
playing 'it's later than you think'
school my last semester will start
and after, I shall leave no job assured
except the Army and no future planned
beyond the summer this summer like
no other I have ever to spend
this last New Year's
I know my mediocrity
I have no ambitions anymore what is ahead
what is ahead I cannot fail I cannot
succeed non sequitur life

PITT POETRY SERIES

COLOPHON

The poems in this book are set in Linotype Times Roman, a typeface designed and cut in 1931 by Stanley Morison for the London *Times*. Although it never became popular in this country as a newspaper typeface, it has met with great favor in the book industry and may be the most popular book typeface in use today. The display face used for the numbers is Torino, a product of Amsterdam Continental based on the old Bodoni designs. The book was printed from the type on Warren's Olde Style paper by Heritage Printers, Inc., and bound in Holliston cloth by John H. Dekker and Sons. The design is by Gary Gore.

DATE DUE